KAHLIL GIBRAN'S
LITTLE BOOK OF WISDOM

KAHLIL GIBRAN'S
LITTLE BOOK OF WISDOM

NEIL DOUGLAS-KLOTZ

AMARYLLIS

AMARYLLIS
An imprint of Manjul Publishing House Pvt. Ltd.
• 7/32, Ansari Road, Daryaganj, New Delhi 110 002
Website: www.manjulindia.com
Registered Office:
• 10, Nishat Colony, Bhopal 462 003 – India

Published by arrangement with
Hampton Roads Publishing Company, Inc., USA.

ISBN 978-93-90085-87-3

Cover design by Manjul Publishing House
Interior by Deborah Dutton, Typeset in ITC Garamond Std

This edition first published in 2021

Printed and bound in India by Thomson Press (India) Ltd.

FOR THOSE WHO LIVE THEIR WISDOM
SIMPLY AND WITHOUT WORDS

Contents

2. Community Wisdom 27

4. A Life Apart: Wisdom from the Solitude 91

5. Wisdom Beyond Words 119

Introduction

> Wisdom: 1) *The quality of being wise, especially in relation to the conduct of means and ends; the combination of experience and knowledge with the ability to apply them judiciously; sound judgment, prudence, practical sense.*

Kahlil Gibran, renowned for a hundred years for his pithy and emotive sayings, the Lebanese-American writer that launched a thousand (or more) greeting cards and wall hangings, never stopped searching for the simple wisdom of how to live a happy and fulfilling life. His deeply emotional search created some of his most memorable writing.

These new "little book" collections take a fresh look at Gibran's words, taking into account the major influences in his life: his Middle Eastern culture, nature mysticism, and the Arabic language in which he thought. One could easily argue that what the average reader of Gibran in the 1920s found exotic was the way he clearly expressed a region that most regarded as a mystery. Nearly a hundred years later, understanding the Middle Eastern (or Southwest Asian) conundrum—especially the way that very different cultures consider the meaning and purpose of life—has shifted from being an early 20th century parlor game to become a practical matter of everyday survival.

The book before you, the fourth and final in the series, gathers Gibran's words on wisdom for daily life, both in community and solitude. The first book collected his writings on life and nature. The second book focused on love and relationships, and the third on life's big questions and the secrets of the spiritual path.

What is a "wise" way to live, either in Gibran's time or ours? Does *wisdom* mean something profound—the province of philosophers, clerics, self-help teachers, psychotherapists, or those with time on their hands to think deep thoughts? Does it mean something subtle, crafty, or devious—the way of the "wise" investor? Back to the dictionary definition above—what would "practical sense" mean today, when so much that we considered both "practical" and "sense" have radically changed in the past decade or two? What are we all looking for in life, anyway?

During his short life (he died at age 48), these questions returned again and again to both fascinate and bedevil Gibran.

This should not be surprising. Kahlil Gibran's adult life began in outer exile. In 1895 his mother Kamileh fled poverty and a failed marriage in Lebanon and brought young Kahlil (age 12), his brother, and two sisters to live in Boston. Today they would be called migrants. Yet Gibran's connection to his native land remained strong throughout his life.

He saw himself as "Syrian" culturally (neither the nations of Syria nor Lebanon existed at the time) and dedicated himself to the liberation of his people from oppressive regimes and systems. During Gibran's youth, political strife engulfed the whole region before, during, and after the First World War. Initially, Gibran had high hopes that the war would dislodge the Ottoman Empire's grip on his homeland. It did this, but Gibran and many others were disappointed by the Sykes-Picot Agreement made by the victorious European and American powers in 1916, before the end of the war, to divide the region into various nation-states for their own benefit.

He poignantly depicts his sense of betrayal in a short ironic parable written during the time about a mother sheep and a lamb watching two eagles fighting above them to determine which would eat them. The story, entitled "War and the Small Nations," ends with the sheep saying to the lamb:

"How strange, my child, that these two noble birds should attack one another. Is not the vast sky large enough for both of them? Pray, my little one, pray in your heart that God may make peace between your winged brothers."

And the lamb prayed in its heart.

Many of the selections in this book express Gibran's trenchant and often prescient views on government, organized religion, wealth, and commerce. As he viewed them, all of these institutions express normal human needs in healthy or unhealthy ways. How consciously or unconsciously people exploit these needs for their own selfish benefit defines how "good" or "evil" the institution may be. As he says in a saying from the collection *Sand and Foam*:

Government is an agreement
between you and myself.
You and myself are often wrong.

That is, Gibran did not recognize any ultimate authority outside the human soul and its direct relationship with "God," a term that he cautions us not to use so casually, or with the presumption that we know what we are actually talking about:

> It were wiser to speak less of God, whom we cannot understand, and more of each other, whom we may understand.
>
> Yet I would have you know that we are the breath and the fragrance of God.
>
> We are God—in leaf, in flower, and oftentimes in fruit.

His critiques of accepted institutions repeatedly led Gibran back to the essential question: how should one live? In trying to answer this, he returns to the paradox that plagued him throughout his life. If living a "normal," simple life produced the most happiness, how does a sensitive person account for the feelings of alienation that separate him or her from those around them? How does one escape this inner exile?

One of Gibran's solutions was to balance solitude with community life, time in spiritual retreat with the increasingly busy life he found in an early 20th century American city. His difficulty finding this balance can be seen in a selection from the book *The Madman* entitled here "I Am Not What I Seem." It begins like this:

> My friend, I am not what I seem.
>
> Seeming is but a garment I wear—a care-woven garment that protects me from your questionings and you from my negligence.
>
> The "I" in me, my friend, dwells in the house of silence, and therein it shall remain forevermore—unperceived, unapproachable.

Resolving his inner alienations—between Lebanese and American culture, between self and community—led Gibran to the major "wisdom" influences of his life: his Middle Eastern Christianity and Sufi mysticism.

As I noted in the introductions to the earlier collections, Gibran was raised as a Maronite Christian, an Eastern church allied to the Roman Catholic but that which until the 18th century spoke and used in liturgy the Syriac language, related directly to Jesus' native Aramaic. The Aramaic-speaking churches historically viewed Jesus, the prophet of Nazareth, as a human being, a small-s "son" of God, who uniquely fulfilled his destiny and expressed the divine life in a way open to all of us. In this sense, we could all become "children" of God, that is, of "Sacred Unity" (the literal translation of the Aramaic word for God, *Alaha*, as well as the equivalent Arabic word *Allah*).

In his 1928 book *Jesus The Son of Man* Gibran introduces us to various figures, Biblical and fictional, who talk about the Jesus they knew. Echoing the above conviction about humanity's potential, the apostle John says:

> Jesus the anointed was the first Word of God uttered unto humanity, even as if one apple

tree in an orchard should bud and blossom a day before the other trees. And in God's orchard, that day was an aeon.

We are all sons and daughters of the Most High, but the anointed one was God's first-born, who dwelt in the body of Jesus of Nazareth.

In writing about the wisdom of how to live, Gibran also draws from the Sufi mystical tradition. Here we find him conveying the Sufi emphasis on "unlearning," that is, the need to release ideas and impressions from the heart and mind before one can enter the heart's depths, the source of love and understanding. Gibran has Almustafa say towards the end of *The Prophet*:

And what is word-knowledge but a shadow
of wordless knowledge?
Wise men have come to you to give you of
their wisdom.
I came to remove your wisdom.

Similarly, in his short story "The Tempest," the narrator meets a hermit who tells him:

> Among all vanities of life, there is only one thing that the spirit loves and craves. . . . It is an awakening in the spirit. It is an awakening in the inner depths of the heart. It is an overwhelming and magnificent power that descends suddenly upon our conscience and opens our eyes. . . . The one who knows it is unable to reveal it by words. And the one who knows it not will never think upon the compelling and beautiful mystery of existence.

Gibran also draws on the ancient Middle Eastern traditions of Holy Wisdom, *Hokhmah* in Hebrew, *Hakima* in Aramaic, better known by her Greek name *Sophia*. Her Semitic language names, also translatable as "Sacred Sense," point to both an archetypal figure as well as an innate ability that enables each of us to make sense of the paradoxes of life as well as the many sense impressions that bombard us every moment.

Identifying with this quality or persona, which many early Christians also associated with Jesus, allowed Gibran to take himself less seriously:

> Wisdom ceases to be wisdom
> when it becomes
> too proud to weep,
> too grave to laugh,
> and too full of its self to
> seek other than itself.

On the actual editing of this book: it is clear that various people helped Gibran with his English grammar and punctuation, particularly his long-time patron, muse and editor Mary Haskell. According to his biographers, Gibran also rarely checked these things after he had written a piece. As the way we read has changed over the past hundred years, so has grammar, so I have re-punctuated or re-lined many selections to bring out the rhythm of Gibran's voice for the modern reader.

As far as Gibran's use of gender-inclusive or exclusive terms go, I have taken a light touch in attempting to preserve his intent, keeping in mind the Arabic language in which he thought. Throughout his writing, Gibran often refers to God as "he," but he also refers to Life or Fortune as "she," and makes frequent references to "goddesses." In the overall picture, things balance out, which is what one finds in reading gendered languages like ancient Hebrew or classical Arabic, where the sun, moon, and various living beings of nature have gendered forms.

In one exception to this editing policy, I have substituted "humanity" for "mankind." This does not disturb the rhythm of Gibran's voice, is more faithful to the underlying (and gender neutral) Arabic word he was thinking of, and is a more accurate way of including us all.

In selecting the material for this book, I have placed well-known sayings of Gibran's next to lesser-known ones. We begin with some of his sayings, short stories, and aphorisms on wending one's way through everyday life. Then we move into Gibran's views on living in community and his critiques of government, the nation state, the legal system, and organized religion. From there we continue to look through his eyes at the natural human need to exchange things: giving and receiving, buying and selling. In the last two sections, we find Gibran's passionate cries from inner and outer solitude, followed by his deeply moving yet paradoxical writing on wisdom beyond words.

This being the final book of the series, I would like to thank Greg Brandenburgh of Red Wheel/Weiser/Hampton Roads Books for his suggestion of and support for this work. Since I first read Gibran's *Jesus The Son of Man* many years ago, I have always held a profound respect for the Lebanese poet and mystic. He navigated a very difficult and conflicted life, harvesting gems of insight and creativity that continue to inspire us more than a hundred years later.

Neil Douglas-Klotz
Fife, Scotland
June 2018

Kahlil Gibran's

Little Book of Wisdom

1

Living a Wise Life

Everyday life offers us many opportunities to make mistakes, learn from experience, and discover wisdom. How can we put what we learn into action in ways that are practical and down-to-earth?

Nirvana

Yes, there is a nirvana.
It is in leading your sheep
to a green pasture,
and in putting your child to sleep,
and in writing the last line of your poem.

To Be a Garden Without Walls

After a space, one of the disciples asked him: "Master, speak to us of *being*. What is it to *be*?"

Almustafa looked long upon him and loved him. And he stood up and walked a distance away from them. Then returning, he said:

In this garden my father and my mother lie, buried by the hands of the living, and in this garden lie buried the seeds of yesteryear, brought here upon the wings of the wind. A thousand times shall my mother and my father be buried here, and a thousand times shall the wind bury the seed.

And a thousand years from now shall you and I and these flowers come together in this garden, even as now. And we shall *be*, loving life, and we shall *be*, dreaming of space, and we shall *be*, rising towards the sun.

But now today, to *be* is to be wise, though not a stranger to the foolish. It is to be strong, but not to the undoing of the weak. To play with young children, not as fathers, but rather as playmates who would learn their games.

To be simple and guileless with old men and women and to sit with them in the shade of the ancient oak-trees, though you are still walking with spring.

To seek a poet, though he may live beyond the seven rivers, and to be at peace in his presence—nothing wanting, nothing doubting, and with no question upon your lips.

To know that the saint and the sinner are twins, whose father is our Gracious King, and that one was born but the moment before the other, wherefore we regard him as the crowned prince.

To follow Beauty even when she leads you to the verge of the precipice. And though she is winged and you are wingless, and though she shall pass beyond the verge, follow her! For where Beauty is not, there is nothing.

To be a garden without walls, a vineyard without a guardian, and a treasure-house forever open to passersby.

There Lived a Man

Long ago there lived a man who was crucified
for being too loving and too lovable.
And strange to relate, I met him thrice yester-
day.
The first time he was asking a policeman not to
take a prostitute to prison.
The second time he was drinking wine with an
outcast.
And the third time he was having a fistfight
with a promoter inside a church.

THE OTHER

If other people laugh at you, you can pity them.
But if you laugh at them, you may never forgive yourself.

If other people injure you, you may forget the injury.
But if you injure them, you will always remember.

In truth the other person is
your most sensitive self
given another body.

Eating and Drinking

Then an old man, a keeper of an inn, said "Speak to us of eating and drinking."

And Almustafa said:

Would that you could live on the fragrance of the earth and be sustained by the light like an air plant.

But since you must kill to eat and rob the newborn of its mother's milk to quench your thirst, let it then be an act of worship.

And let your table stand as an altar on which the pure and the innocent of forest and plain are sacrificed for that which is purer and still more innocent in a human being.

When you kill a beast, say to it in your heart, "By the same power that slays you, I too am slain, and I too shall be consumed. For the law that delivered you into my hand shall deliver me into a mightier hand. Your blood and my blood is nothing but the sap that feeds the tree of heaven."

When you crush an apple with your teeth, say to it in your heart, "Your seeds shall live in my body, and the buds of your tomorrow shall blossom in my heart. Your fragrance shall be my breath, and together we shall rejoice through all the seasons."

In the autumn, when you gather the grapes of your vineyard for the winepress, say in your heart, "I too am a vineyard, and my fruit shall be gathered for the winepress. And like new wine, I shall be kept in eternal vessels."

In winter, when you draw the wine, let there be in your heart a song for each cup. And let there be in the song a remembrance for the autumn days, for the vineyard, and for the winepress.

Gatekeeper of Your Necessities

They wonder that he who said
"My kingdom is not of this earth" also said
"Render unto Caesar that which is Caesar's."

Yet they do not know that
if they would be free to enter
the kingdom of their passion,
they must not resist
the gatekeeper of their necessities.

It behooves them to
gladly pay the price to
enter into that city.

When You Work with Love

You have also been told that
life is darkness,
and in your weariness
you echo what was said
by the weary.

And I say that
life is indeed darkness,
save when there is urge.
And all urge is blind,
save when there is knowledge.
And all knowledge is vain,
save when there is work.
And all work is empty,
save when there is love.

When you work with love
you bind yourself to yourself
and to one another
and to God.

The Wisdom of Critics

One nightfall a man traveling on horseback towards the sea reached an inn by the roadside.

He dismounted and, trusting people and night like all riders towards the sea, tied his horse to a tree beside the door and entered into the inn.

At midnight, when all were asleep, a thief came and stole the traveler's horse.

In the morning the man awoke and discovered that his horse was stolen. He grieved for his horse and that a man had found it in his heart to steal.

Then his fellow lodgers came and stood around him and began to talk.

The first man said, "How foolish of you to tie your horse outside the stable."

And the second said, "Still more foolish, without even hobbling the horse."

And the third man said, "It is stupid at best to travel to the sea on horseback."

And the fourth said, "Only the indolent and the slow of foot own horses."

Then the traveler was much astonished.

At last he cried, "My friends, because my horse was stolen, you have hastened one and all to tell me my faults and my shortcomings. But strange, not one word of reproach have you uttered about the man who stole my horse!"

The Scholar and the Poet

There lies a green field between
the scholar and the poet.
Should the scholar cross it,
he becomes a wise man.
Should the poet cross it,
he becomes a prophet.

The Mask of Wit

Wit is often a mask.

If you could tear it away,
you would find either
a genius irritated or
cleverness juggling.

And only when jugglers miss
catching the ball
do they appeal to me.

Professional Talkers

The most talkative is the least intelligent, and there is hardly a difference between an orator and an auctioneer.

Being Candid

If indeed you must be candid,
be candid beautifully.

Otherwise keep silent,
for there is a person
in our neighborhood
who is dying.

Ancestry

Every person is the descendant of
every king and every slave
that ever lived.

If the great-grandfather of Jesus
had known what was
hidden within him,
would he not have stood
in awe of himself?

The Children of Tomorrow

The children of yesterday are walking in the funeral of an era that they created for themselves. They are pulling a rotted rope that might break soon and cause them to drop into a forgotten abyss.

They are living in homes with weak foundations. As the storm blows—and it is about to blow—their homes will fall upon their heads and so become their tombs.

I say that all their thoughts, sayings, quarrels, compositions, and books—all their work—are nothing but chains dragging them down, because they are too weak to pull the load.

But the children of tomorrow are the ones called by life, and they follow life with steady steps and heads high.

They are the dawn of new frontiers. No smoke will veil their eyes, and no jingle of chains will drown out their voices.

They are few in number, but the difference is as between a grain of wheat and a stack of hay.

No one knows them, but they know each other.

They are like the summits of mountains, which can see or hear each other—not like the caves, which cannot hear or see.

They are the seed dropped by the hand of God in the field, breaking through its pod and waving its sapling leaves before the face of the sun.

It shall grow into a mighty tree, its root in the heart of the earth and its branches high in the sky.

Your Children

A woman who held a babe against her bosom said, "Speak to us of children." And Almustafa said:

Your children are not your children.
They are the sons and daughters of
life's longing for itself.

They come through you
but not from you.
And though they are with you,
they belong not to you.

You may give them your love
but not your thoughts,
for they have their own thoughts.

You may house their bodies
but not their souls,
for their souls dwell in
the house of tomorrow,
which you cannot visit—
not even in your dreams.

You may strive to be like them,
but do not seek to make them like you.
For life goes not backward
nor tarries with yesterday.

You are the bows from which
your children, as living arrows,
are sent forth.

The Archer sees the mark
upon the path of the infinite,
and bends you with his might
that the arrows may go swift and far.
Let your bending
in the Archer's hand
be for gladness.

For even as he loves
the arrow that flies,
so he loves also
the bow that is stable.

The Best Sacrifice

The disciple Matthew recalls sayings from Jesus' "Sermon on the Mount":

"You have been charged by the ancients to bring your calf, your lamb, and your dove to the temple and to slay them upon the altar, that the nostrils of God may feed upon the odor of their fat, and that you may be forgiven your failings.

"But I say unto you, would you give God that which was God's own from the beginning? And would you appease the One whose throne is above the silent deep and whose arms encircle space?

"Rather, seek out your brother and sister and be reconciled unto them before you seek the temple. And be a loving giver unto your neighbor.

"For in the soul of these God has built a temple that shall not be destroyed, and in their hearts God has raised an altar that shall never perish.

Speaking Less of God

And Almustafa said to them:

You would rise up in fancy to the clouds, and you deem it height. And you would pass over the vast sea and claim it to be distance.

But I say unto you that when you sow a seed in the earth, you reach a greater height. And when you hail the beauty of the morning to your neighbor, you cross a greater sea.

Too often do you sing of God the infinite, and yet in truth you do not hear the song.

Would that you might listen to the song-birds, and to the leaves that forsake the branch when the wind passes by. And do not forget, my friends, that these sing only when they are separated from the branch!

Again I bid you to speak not so freely of God, who is your All, but rather speak and understand one another, neighbor to neighbor, a god unto a god.

It is only when you are lost in your smaller selves that you seek the sky that you call "God."

Would that you might find paths into your vast selves! Would that you might be less idle and pave the roads!

It were wiser to speak less of God, whom we cannot understand, and more of each other, whom we might understand.

Yet I would have you know that we are the breath and the fragrance of God.

We are God—in leaf, in flower, and oftentimes in fruit.

2

Community Wisdom

People naturally group together in communities as do many other species. How do we create associations that benefit us, rather than place us in chains—in body or thought? What would a healthy government, religious organization, legal system, or nation-state actually look like?

GOVERNMENT

Government is an agreement
between you and me.
You and I are often wrong.

The true prince is the one
who finds his throne
in the heart of the dervish.

BETWEEN THE FROWN OF THE TIGER AND THE SMILE OF THE WOLF

Since the beginning of creation and up to our present time, certain clans, rich by inheritance, in cooperation with the clergy, have appointed themselves the administrators of the people. It is an old, gaping wound in the heart of society that cannot be removed except by the intense removal of ignorance.

The one who acquires wealth by inheritance builds a mansion with the weak poor's money. The clergy erect their temples upon the graves and bones of their devoted worshippers.

The prince grasps the *fellahin's*[1] arms while the priest empties their pockets. The ruler looks upon the children of the fields with a frowning face, and the bishop consoles them with his smile.

1. *Fellahin,* Arabic: farmers or agricultural workers. During the Ottoman period, which was that described by Gibran, the word *fellah* could also refer to a landless villager or "peasant," as opposed to a member of the land-owning class.

And between the frown of the tiger and the smile of the wolf, the flock perishes.

The ruler claims himself as king of the law and the priest as the representative of God, and between these two, bodies are destroyed and souls wither into nothing.

Inherited Spiritual Disease

Human society has yielded for seventy centuries to corrupted laws, until it cannot understand the meaning of superior and eternal laws.

A person's eyes that have become accustomed to the dim light of candles cannot see the sunlight.

Spiritual disease is inherited from one generation to another until it becomes a part of people, who look upon it not as a disease but as a natural gift showered by God upon Adam.

If those people found someone free from the germs of this disease, they would think of him with shame and disgrace.

Good Government

The people of the Kingdom of Sadik surrounded the palace of their king, shouting in rebellion against him. And he came down the steps of the palace, carrying his crown in one hand and his scepter in the other.

The majesty of his appearance silenced the multitude, and he stood before them and said, "My friends, who are no longer my subjects, here I yield my crown and scepter unto you. I would be one of you. I am only one man, but as a man I would work together with you that our lot may be made better. There is no need for a king. Let us go therefore to the fields and the vineyards and labor, hand in hand. Only you must tell me to what field or vineyard I should go. All of you now are king."

The people marvelled, and stillness was upon them for the king whom they had deemed the source of their discontent now yielded his crown and scepter to them and became as one of them.

Then each and every one of them went his way, and the king walked with one man to a field.

But the Kingdom of Sadik did not fare better without a king, and the mist of discontent was still upon the land. The people cried out in the marketplaces saying that they wanted to be governed and that they would have a king to rule them. And the elders and the youths said, as if with one voice, "We will have our king!"

So they sought the king and found him toiling in the field. They brought him to his seat and yielded to him his crown and scepter. And they said, "Now rule us, with might and with justice."

And he said, "I will indeed rule you with might, and may the gods of the heaven and the earth help me that I may also rule with justice."

Now there came into his presence men and women who spoke to him of a baron who mistreated them and to whom they were but serfs.

And straightway the king brought the baron before him and said, "The life of one man is as weighty in the scales of God as the life of another. And because you know not how to weigh the lives of those who work in your fields and your vineyards, you are banished and you shall leave this kingdom forever."

The following day came another company to the king and spoke of the cruelty of a countess beyond the hills and how she brought them down to misery. Instantly the countess was brought to court, and the king sentenced her also to banishment saying, "Those who till our fields and care for our vineyards are nobler than we who eat the bread they prepare and drink the wine of their winepress. And because you do not know this, you shall leave this land and live far from this kingdom."

Then came men and women who said that the bishop made them bring and hew stones for the cathedral, yet he gave them nothing though they knew the bishop's coffer was full of gold and silver while they themselves were empty with hunger.

And the king called for the bishop, and when the bishop came, the king said to him, "That cross you wear upon your bosom should mean giving life unto life. But you have taken life from life, and you have given none. Therefore you shall leave this kingdom never to return."

Thus each day for a full moon men and women came to the king to tell him of the burdens laid upon them. And each and every day for a full moon some oppressor was exiled from the land.

And the people of Sadik were amazed, and there was cheer in their hearts.

And one day the elders and the youths came and surrounded the tower of the king and called for him. And he came down holding his crown in one hand and his scepter in the other.

And he asked, "Now what do you want of me? Behold, I yield back to you that which you desired me to hold."

But they cried, "No, no, you are our rightful king. You have made clean the land of vipers, and you have brought the wolves to naught, and we come to sing our thanksgiving to you. The crown is yours in majesty, and the scepter is yours in glory."

Then the king said, "Not I, not I. You yourselves are king. When you deemed me weak and a misruler, you yourselves were weak and misruling. And now the land fares well because it is in your will. I am but a thought in the mind of you all, and I do not exist except in your actions. There is no such person as a governor. Only the governed exist to govern themselves."

And the king reentered his tower with his crown and his scepter. And the elders and the youths went their various ways and were content.

And all thought of themselves as a king with a crown in one hand and a scepter in the other.

Busy Cattle

A rebellious monk speaks to his elders:

Why are you living in the shadow of parasitism, segregating yourselves from the people who are in need of knowledge? Why are you depriving the country of your help?

Jesus has sent you as lambs among the wolves. What has made you as wolves among the lambs? Why are you fleeing from humanity and from God who created you?

If you are better than the people who walk in the procession of life, you should go to them and better their lives. But if you think they are better than you, you should desire to learn from them.

How do you take an oath and vow to live in poverty, then forget what you have vowed and live in luxury? How do you swear obedience to God and then revolt against all that religion means? How do you adopt virtue as your rule when your hearts are full of lust?

You pretend that you are killing your bodies, but in fact you are killing your souls. You pretend to abhor earthly things, but your hearts are swollen with greed. You would have the people believe in you as religious teachers. Truly speaking, you are like busy cattle who divert themselves from knowledge by grazing in a green and beautiful pasture.

Let us restore to the needy the vast land of the convent and give back to them the silver and gold we took from them. Let us disperse from our aloofness and serve the weak, who made us strong, and cleanse the country in which we live. Let us teach this miserable nation to smile and rejoice with heaven's bounty and with the glory of life and freedom!

The One Thousand Laws

Ages ago there was a great king who was wise. And he desired to enact laws for his subjects.

He called one thousand wise men from one thousand different tribes to his capital to lay down the laws.

And all this came to pass.

But when one thousand laws written upon parchment were put before the king and he read them, he wept bitterly in his soul, for he had not known that there were one thousand forms of crime in his kingdom.

Then he called his scribe, and with a smile on his face, he himself dictated laws. And his laws were but seven.

And the one thousand wise men left him in anger and returned to their tribes with the laws they had laid down. And every tribe followed the laws of its wise men.

Therefore they have one thousand laws even to our own day.

It is a great country, but it has one thousand prisons, and the prisons are full of women and men, breakers of a thousand laws.

It is indeed a great country, but its people are the descendants of one thousand lawgivers and only one wise king.

The Criminal

A young man of strong body, weakened by hunger, sat on the walker's portion of the street stretching his hand toward all who passed, begging and repeating the sad song of his defeat in life, while suffering from hunger and humiliation.

When night came, his lips and tongue were parched, while his hand was still as empty as his stomach.

He gathered himself and went out of the city, where he sat under a tree and wept bitterly. Then he lifted his puzzled eyes to heaven, while hunger was eating his insides, and said,

"O Lord, I went to the rich man and asked for employment, but he turned me away because of my shabbiness. I knocked at the school door, but was forbidden solace, because I was empty-handed. I sought any occupation that would give me bread, but all to no avail. In desperation, I asked alms, but the worshippers saw me and said "He is strong and lazy, and he should not beg."

"O Lord, it is thy will that my mother gave birth unto me, and now the earth offers me back to You before the ending."

Then his expression changed. He arose, and his eyes now glittered in determination. He fashioned a thick and heavy stick from the branch of the tree and pointed it toward the city, shouting, "I asked for bread with all the strength of my voice and was refused. Now I shall obtain it by the strength of my muscles! I asked for bread in the name of mercy and love, but humanity did not listen. I shall now take it in the name of evil!"

The passing years rendered the youth a robber, a killer, and a destroyer of souls. He crushed all who opposed him. He amassed fabulous wealth with which he won himself over to those in power. He was admired by colleagues, envied by other thieves, and feared by the multitudes.

His riches and false position prevailed upon the emir to appoint him deputy in that city—the sad process pursued by unwise governors. Thefts were then legalized. Oppression was supported by authority. Crushing of the weak became commonplace, the throngs curried his favor and praised him.

Thus does the first touch of humanity's selfishness make criminals of the humble and make killers of the sons of peace.

Thus does the early greed of humanity grow and strike back at humanity a thousandfold.

Your Thought and Mine

Your thought is a tree rooted deep in the soil of tradition, whose branches grow in the power of continuity. My thought is a cloud moving in space. It turns into drops which as they fall, form a brook that sings its way to the sea. Then it rises as vapor into the sky.

Your thought is a fortress that neither gale nor lightning can shake. My thought is a tender leaf that sways in every direction and finds pleasure in its swaying.

Your thought is an ancient dogma that cannot change you nor can you change it. My thought is new. It tests me and I test it, morning and evening.

You have your thought, and I have mine.

Your thought advocates Judaism, Brahmanism, Buddhism, Christianity, and Islam. In my thought there is only one universal religion, whose varied paths are but the fingers of the loving hand of the Supreme Being.

In your thought there are the rich, the poor, and the beggared. My thought holds that there are no riches but life, that we are all beggars, and no benefactor exists save life herself.

You have your thought, and I have mine.

According to your thought, the greatness of nations lies in their politics, parties, conferences, alliances, and treaties. But mine proclaims that the importance of nations lies in work—work in the field, in the vineyards, with the loom, in the tannery, in the quarry, in the timberyard, in the office, and in the press.

Your thought holds that the glory of nations is in their heroes. It sings the praises of Rameses, Alexander, Caesar, Hannibal, and Napoleon. But mine claims that the real heroes are Confucius, Lao-Tzu, Socrates, Plato, Abu Talib, Al-Ghazali, Jelaluddin Rumi, Copernicus, and Pasteur.

Your thought sees power in armies, cannons, battleships, submarines, airplanes, and poison gas. But mine asserts that power lies in reason, resolution, and truth. No matter how long the tyrant endures, he will be the loser at the end.

Your thought differentiates between the pragmatist and the idealist, between the part and the whole, between the mystic and the materialist. Mine realizes that life is one, and its weights, measures, and tables do not coincide with your weights, measures, and tables. The one whom you suppose an idealist may be a practical person.

You have your thought, and I have mine.

War and the Small Nations (1920)

Once, high above a pasture where a sheep and a lamb were grazing, an eagle was circling and gazing hungrily down upon the lamb. And as it was about to descend and seize its prey, another eagle appeared and hovered above the sheep and her young with the same hungry intent. Then the two rivals began to fight, filling the sky with their fierce cries.

The sheep looked up and was much astonished. She turned to the lamb and said, "How strange, my child, that these two noble birds should attack one another. Is not the vast sky large enough for both of them? Pray, my little one, pray in your heart that God may make peace between your winged brothers."

And the lamb prayed in its heart.

History and the Shepherdess (1914-1918)

By the side of a rivulet that meandered among the rocks at the foot of Lebanon's mountains sat a shepherdess, surrounded by her flock of lean sheep grazing upon dry grass. She looked into the distant twilight as if the future were passing before her. Tears had jeweled her eyes like dew-drops adorning flowers. Sorrow had caused her lips to open, so that it might enter and occupy her sighing heart.

After sunset, as the knolls and hills wrapped themselves in shadow, History stood before the maiden. He was an old man whose white hair fell like snow over his breast and shoulders, and in his right hand he held a sharp sickle. In a voice like the roaring sea he said, "Peace unto you, Syria."

The virgin rose trembling with fear. "What do you wish of me, History?" she asked. Then she pointed to her sheep. "This is the remnant of a healthy flock that once filled this valley. This is all that your covetousness has left me. Have you come now to sate your greed on that?

"These plains that were once so fertile have been trodden to barren dust by your trampling feet. My cattle that once grazed upon flowers and produced rich milk now gnaw at thistles that leave them gaunt and dry.

"Fear God, O History, and afflict me no more! The sight of you has made me detest life, and the cruelty of your sickle has caused me to love Death.

"Leave me in my solitude to drain the cup of sorrow, my best wine. Go, History, to the West, where life's wedding feast is being celebrated. Here let me lament the bereavement you have prepared for me."

Concealing his sickle under the folds of his garment, History looked upon her as a loving father looks upon his child and said, "O Syria, what I have taken from you were my own gifts. Know that your sister nations are entitled to a part of the glory that was yours. I must give to them what I gave you. Your plight is like that of Egypt, Persia, and Greece, for each one of them also has a lean flock and dry pasture. O Syria, that which you call degradation is an indispensable sleep from which you will draw strength. The flower does not return to life save through death, and love does not grow except after separation."

The old man came close to the maiden, stretched forth his hand, and said, "Shake my hand, O Daughter of the Prophets."

And she shook his hand and looked at him from behind a screen of tears and said, "Farewell, History, farewell."

And he responded, "Until we meet again Syria, until we meet again."

And the old man disappeared like swift lightning, and the shepherdess called her sheep and started on her way, saying to herself, "Shall there be another meeting?"

Pity the Nation

Pity the nation
that wears a cloth it does not weave,
that eats a bread it does not harvest,
that drinks a wine that flows not
from its own winepress.

Pity the nation
that acclaims the bully a hero,
and that deems the glittering conqueror
bountiful.
Pity the nation
that despises passion in its dreaming,
yet submits meekly in its awakening.

Pity the nation
that does not raise its voice
except when it walks in a funeral,
that does not boast except among its ruins,
and that will not rebel
save when its neck is laid
between the sword and the block.

Pity the nation
whose statesman is a fox,
whose philosopher is a juggler,
and whose art is that
of patching and mimicking.

Pity the nation
that welcomes its new ruler with trumpetings,
and farewells him with hootings,
only to welcome another with trumpetings
again.

The New Frontiers (1925)

There is in the Middle East an awakening that defies slumber. This awakening will conquer, because the sun is its leader and the dawn is its army.

In the fields of the Middle East, which have been a large burial ground, stand the youth of spring calling the occupants of the sepulchers to rise and march toward the new frontiers.

When the spring sings its hymns, the dead of the winter rise, shed their shrouds, and march forward.

Come and tell me who and what you are.

Are you a politician asking what your country can do for you or a zealous one asking what you can do for your country? If you are the first, then you are a parasite. If the second, then you are an oasis in a desert.

Are you a merchant using the need of society for the necessities of life for your own monopoly and exorbitant profit? Or are you a sincere, hard-working, and diligent person facilitating the exchange between the weaver and the farmer and charging a reasonable profit as a broker between supply and demand? If you are the first, then you are a criminal, whether you live in a palace or a prison. If you are the second, then you are a charitable person, whether you are thanked or denounced by people.

Are you a religious leader, weaving for your body a gown out of the ignorance of the people, fashioning a crown out of the simplicity of their hearts, and pretending to hate the devil merely to live upon his income?

Or are you a devout, pious person who sees in the piety of the individual the foundation for a progressive nation and who can see, through a profound search in the depth of your own soul, a ladder to the eternal soul that directs the world?

If you are the first, then you are a heretic, a disbeliever in God, even if you fast by day and pray by night.

If you are the second, then you are a violet in the garden of truth. Even if your fragrance is lost upon the nostrils of humanity, yet your aroma rises into that rare air where the fragrance of flowers is preserved.

O Liberty

O Liberty! Have mercy on us!

Before your great throne we stand, the blood-stained garments of our ancestors hanging on our bodies, our heads covered with the dust of their graves mixed with their remains, carrying the swords that stabbed their hearts, lifting the spears that pierced their bodies, dragging the chains that slowed their feet, uttering the cries that wounded their throats, lamenting and repeating the songs of our failure that echoed throughout the prison, and repeating the prayers that came from the depths of our ancestors' hearts.

Listen to us, O Liberty, and hear us!

From the Nile to the Euphrates comes the wailing of the suffering souls, in unison with the cry of the abyss. From the end of the East to the mountains of Lebanon, hands are stretched to you, trembling with the presence of death. From the shores of the sea to the end of the desert, tear-flooded eyes look beseechingly toward you.

Come, O Liberty, and save us!

In the wretched huts standing in the shadow of poverty and oppression, they beat their bosoms, soliciting your mercy. Watch us, O Liberty, and have mercy on us. In the pathways and in the houses, miserable youth calls you. In the churches and the mosques, the forgotten holy books turn to you. In the courts and in the palaces, the neglected law appeals to you.

Have mercy on us, O Liberty, and save us!

In our narrow streets the merchants sell their days in order to earn tribute for the exploiting thieves of the West, and none would give them advice. In the barren fields the *fellahin* till the soil, sow the seeds of their hearts, and nourish them with their tears. But they reap nothing except thorns, and none would teach them the true path. In our arid plains, the Bedouin roam barefoot and hungry, but none would have mercy upon them.

Speak, O Liberty, and teach us!

Our sick lambs are grazing upon the grassless prairie, our calves are gnawing on the roots of the trees, and our horses are feeding on dry plants.

Come, O Liberty, and help us!

We have been living in darkness since the beginning. Like prisoners they take us from one prison to another while time ridicules our plight. When will dawn come? How long shall we bear the scorn of the ages?

Many a stone have we been dragging, and many a yoke has been placed upon our necks. How long shall we bear this inhuman outrage? The Egyptian slavery, the Babylon exile, the tyranny of Persia, the despotism of the Romans, and the greed of Europe: all these things have we suffered.

Where are we going now, and when shall we reach the sublime end of the rough roadway? From the clutches of Pharaoh to the paws of Nebuchadnezzar to the iron hands of Alexander to the swords of Herod to the talons of Nero and the sharp teeth of Demon—into whose hands are we now to fall? When will death come and take us, so we may rest at last?

With the strength of our arms we lifted the columns of the temple, and upon our backs we carried the mortar to build the great walls and the impregnable pyramids for the sake of glory. How long shall we continue building such magnificent palaces while living in wretched huts? How long shall we continue filling the bins of the rich with provisions, while sustaining weak life on dry morsels? How long shall we continue weaving silk and wool for our lords and masters while we wear nothing except tattered rags?

Through their wickedness we were divided among ourselves. In order to keep their thrones and be at ease, they armed the Druze to fight the Arab, and stirred up the Shiite to attack the Sunni, and encouraged the Kurd to butcher the Bedouin, and cheered the Muslim to dispute with the Christian.

How long shall brothers and sisters continue to kill their own family upon their mother's bosom? How long shall the cross be kept apart from the crescent before the eyes of God?

O Liberty, hear us! Speak on behalf of but one individual, for a great fire is started with a small spark.

O Liberty, awaken but one heart with the rustling of your wings, for from one cloud alone comes the lightning that illuminates the pits of the valleys and the tops of the mountains.

Disperse with your power these black clouds. Descend like thunder and destroy the thrones that were built upon the bones and skulls of our ancestors.

Hear us, O Liberty!
Bring mercy, O Daughter of Athens!
Rescue us, O Sister of Rome!
Advise us, O Companion of Moses!
Help us, O Beloved of Muhammad!
Teach us, O Bride of Jesus!
Strengthen our hearts so we may live.
Or harden our enemies so we may perish
and live in peace eternally.

A Throne Beyond Your Vision

James the son of Zebedee remembers Jesus' sayings:

"My face and your faces shall not be masked. Our hand shall hold neither sword nor scepter, and our subjects shall love us in peace and shall not be in fear of us."

Thus spoke Jesus, and unto all the kingdoms of the earth I was blinded, unto all the cities of walls and towers. And it was in my heart to follow the master to his kingdom.

Then just at that moment, Judas of Iscariot stepped forth. And he walked up to Jesus and said, "Behold, the kingdoms of the world are vast, and behold, the cities of David and Solomon shall prevail against the Romans. If you will be the king of the Jews, we shall stand beside you with sword and shield, and we shall overcome the alien."

But when Jesus heard this, he turned upon Judas, and his face was filled with wrath. He spoke in a voice as terrible as the thunder of the sky and he said, "Get you behind me, Satan! Do you think that I came down the years to rule an anthill for a day?

"My throne is a throne beyond your vision. Shall he whose wings encircle the earth seek shelter in a nest abandoned and forgotten?

"Shall the living be honored and exalted by the wearers of shrouds?

"My kingdom is not of this earth, and my seat is not built upon the skulls of your ancestors.

"If you seek anything except the kingdom of the spirit then it were better for you to leave me here and go down to the caves of your dead, where the crowned heads of yore hold court in their tombs and may still be bestowing honors upon the bones of your forefathers.

"Dare you tempt me with a crown of dross, when my forehead seeks either the Pleiades or else your thorns?

"Were it not for a dream dreamed by a forgotten race I would not suffer your sun to rise upon my patience, nor your moon to throw my shadow across your path.

"Were it not for a mother's desire, I would have stripped me of the swaddling clothes and escaped back to space.

"And were it not for the sorrow in all of you, I would not have stayed to weep.

"Who are you and what are you, Judas Iscariot? And why do you tempt me?

"Have you in truth weighed me in the scale and found me one to lead legions of pygmies and to direct chariots of the shapeless against an enemy that encamps only in your hatred and marches nowhere but in your fear?

"Too many are the worms that crawl about my feet, and I will give them no battle. I am weary of the jest, and weary of pitying the creepers who deem me a coward because I will not move among their guarded walls and towers.

"Pity it is that I must needs pity to the very end. Would that I could turn my steps towards a larger world where larger beings dwell. But how shall I?

"Your priest and your emperor would have my blood. They shall be satisfied before I go hence. I would not change the course of the law. And I would not govern folly.

"Let ignorance reproduce itself, until it is weary of its own offspring.

"Let the blind lead the blind to the pitfall.

"And let the dead bury the dead, till the earth be choked with its own bitter fruit.

"My kingdom is not of the earth. My kingdom shall be where two or three of you shall meet in love, and in wonder at the loveliness of life, and in good cheer, and in remembrance of me."

3

Wise Exchanges

Our relationships are rooted in exchanges between one another. Is there such a thing as an ethical exchange? What is something actually worth? Is a just economic system possible? Is it really better to give than to receive? What is real generosity?

A Gracious Wolf

Said a gracious wolf to a simple sheep,
"Will you not honor our house with a visit?"
And the sheep answered,
"We would be honored to visit your house
if it were not in your stomach."

CREDIT

We often borrow from our tomorrows
to pay debts to our yesterdays.

POMEGRANATES

There was once a man who had many pomegranate trees in his orchard. And for many an autumn he would put his pomegranates on silver trays outside of his dwelling. Upon the trays he would place signs on which he had written, "Take one for free. You are welcome."

But people passed by, and no one took the fruit.

Then the man thought again, and one autumn he placed no pomegranates on silver trays outside of his dwelling, but he raised a sign in large lettering:

"Here we have the best pomegranates in the land, and we sell them for more silver than any other pomegranates."

And now, behold, all the people of the neighborhood came rushing to buy.

A Prison of Wealth

In some countries the parents' wealth is a source of misery for their children.

The wide, strong box that the father and mother together have used for the safety of their wealth becomes a narrow, dark prison for the souls of their heirs.

The Almighty Dinar that people worship becomes a demon that punishes the spirit and deadens the heart.

The Song of True Fortune

Humanity and I are sweethearts.
It craves me and I long for it,
but alas—between us has appeared
a rival who brings us misery.

She is cruel and demanding,
possessing empty allure.
Her name is property.
She follows wherever we go
and watches like a sentinel,
bringing restlessness to my lover.

I seek my beloved humanity
in the forest,
under the trees,
by the lakes.

But I cannot find it,
for property has spirited it away
to the clamorous city and
placed it on a throne
of quaking, metal riches.

I call for humanity with
the voice of knowledge
and the song of wisdom.
But humanity does not listen,
for property has enticed it
into a dungeon of selfishness
where avarice dwells.

I seek humanity in
the field of contentment,
but I am alone,
for my rival has imprisoned it
in a cave of gluttony and greed
and locked it there with
painful chains of gold.

I call to humanity at dawn
when nature smiles,
but it does not hear,
for excess has laden its drugged eyes
with sick slumber.

I beguile it at eventide
when silence rules and
the flowers sleep.
But humanity does not respond,
for its fear about what
the morrow will bring
shadows its thoughts.

Humanity yearns to love me.
It asks for me in its own acts,
but it will not find me
except in God's acts.

Humanity seeks me in
the edifices of glory
that it has built upon
the bones of others.

Humanity whispers to me
from among its heaps
of gold and silver,
but it will find me
only by coming to
the house of simplicity,
which God has built
at the brink of
the stream of affection.

Humanity desires to
kiss me in front of its coffers,
but its lips will never touch mine
except in the richness
of the pure breeze.

Humanity asks me to
share in its fabulous wealth,
but I will not forsake God's fortune.
I will not cast off my cloak of beauty.

It seeks deceit as a medium, but
I seek only the medium of its heart.
It bruises its own heart in a narrow cell.
I would enrich its heart with all my love.

My beloved has learned how to
shriek and cry for my enemy,
property.

I would teach it how to shed
tears of affection and mercy
from the eyes of its soul
for all things,
and to utter sighs of contentment
through those tears.

VALUE

Once a man unearthed in his field a marble statue of great beauty. He took it to a collector who loved beautiful things and offered it to him for sale. And the collector bought it for a large price, and they parted.

As the man walked home with his money, he thought to himself, "How much life this money means! How could anyone give all this for a dead, carved stone, buried and undreamed of in the earth for a thousand years?"

And at the same time the collector was looking at the statue and thinking to himself, "What beauty! What life! The dream of what a soul! And fresh with the sweet sleep of a thousand years. How could anyone give all this for money, dead and dreamless?"

In the Marketplace

When you toilers of the sea and fields and vineyards meet the weavers and the potters and the gatherers of spices in the marketplace:

Invoke then the master-spirit of the earth to come into your midst and sanctify the scales and the reckoning that weighs value against value.

And do not permit the barren-handed to take part in your transactions, those who would sell only their words for your labor.

To such you should say, "Come with us to the field, or go with our brothers and sisters to the sea and cast your nets. For the land and the sea shall be bountiful to you even as to us."

And if there come singers and dancers and flute-players, buy their gifts also. For they too are gatherers of fruit and frankincense. And that which they bring, though fashioned of dreams, is raiment and food for your soul.

And before you leave the marketplace, see that no one has gone away with empty hands.

For the master-spirit of the earth shall not sleep peacefully upon the wind until the needs of the least of you are satisfied.

Giving Without Looking in a Mirror

You give much and
know not that you give at all.

Verily, the kindness that
gazes upon itself in a mirror
turns to stone.

And a good deed that calls itself
by tender names becomes
the parent to a curse.

Generosity and Pride

Generosity is giving more than you can.
Pride is taking less than you need.

Giving as the Myrtle Breathes

Then said a rich man, "Speak to us of giving."
And Almustafa answered:

You give but little
when you give of your possessions.
It is when you give of yourself
that you truly give.

For what are your possessions but
things you keep and guard
for fear you may need them tomorrow?

And tomorrow,
what shall tomorrow bring
to the over-prudent dog, burying bones
in the trackless sand as it follows
the pilgrims to the holy city?

And what is fear of need
but need itself?
Is not dread of thirst
when your well is full
the thirst that is unquenchable?

There are those who give little
of the much that they have—
and they give it for recognition.
And their hidden desire
makes their gifts unwholesome.

And there are those who have little
and give it all.
These are the believers in life
and the bounty of life,
and their coffers are never empty.

There are those who give with joy,
and that joy is their reward.
And there are those who give with pain,
and that pain is their baptism.

There are those who give
and do not know pain in giving,
nor do they seek joy
nor give with mindfulness of virtue.

They give as in yonder valley
the myrtle breathes
its fragrance into space.
Through the hands of such as these
God speaks,
and from behind their eyes
God smiles upon the earth.

It is well to give when asked,
but it is better to give unasked,
through understanding.
And to the open-handed
the search for one who shall receive
is joy greater than giving.

And is there anything you would withhold?
All you have shall someday be given.
Therefore give now,
that the season of giving may be yours
and not your inheritors.

You often say,
"I would give, but only to the deserving."
The trees in your orchard do not say so,
nor the flocks in your pasture.
They give that they may live,
for to withhold is to perish.

Surely the ones who are worthy
to receive their days and nights
are worthy of all else from you.
And those who have deserved to drink
from the ocean of life deserve to
fill their cups from your little stream.

And what greater deserving shall there be
than that which lies in the courage
and the confidence, nay the charity,
of receiving?

And who are you
that people should rend their bosoms
and unveil their pride,
that you may see their worth naked
and their pride unabashed?

See first that you yourself
deserve to be a giver
and an instrument of giving.

For in truth it is life
that gives unto life—
while you,
who deem yourself a giver,
are but a witness.

And you receivers—
and you are all receivers—
assume no weight of gratitude,
lest you lay a yoke upon yourself
and upon him who gives.

Rather, rise together with the giver
on the wings of the gifts.
For to be over-mindful of your debt
is to doubt the generosity of the giver,
who has the free-hearted earth for mother,
and God for father.

Generosity

Those who give you a serpent
when you ask for a fish,
may have nothing but serpents to give.

It is then generosity on their part.

None to Receive

It is indeed misery
if I stretch an empty hand
to humanity and receive nothing.

But it is hopelessness
if I stretch a full hand
and find no one to receive.

Giving for Those in Need

[An appeal for famine relief for the people of Syria (and by extension Lebanon, which was not yet a nation-state) during the First World War:]

My people and your people, my Syrian brothers and sisters, are dead.

What can be done for those who are dying?

Our lamentations will not satisfy their hunger, and our tears will not quench their thirst.

What can we do to save them between the iron paws of hunger?

My brothers and sisters, the kindness that compels you to give a part of your life to any human beings who are in the shadow of losing their lives is the only virtue that makes you worthy of the light of day and the peace of the night.

Remember, my brothers and sisters, that the coin that you drop into the withered hand stretching toward you is the only golden chain that binds your rich heart to the loving heart of God.

The House of Real Fortune

My wearied heart bade me farewell and left for the house of fortune. As it reached that holy city, which the soul had blessed and worshipped, it commenced wondering. For my heart could not find what it had always imagined would be there. The city was empty of power, money, and authority.

And my heart spoke to the daughter of love saying, "Oh love, where can I find contentment? I heard that she had come here to join you."

And the daughter of love responded, "Contentment has already gone to preach her gospel in the city, where greed and corruption are paramount. We are not in need of her."

Real fortune craves not contentment, which is an earthly hope, its desires embraced by union with objects.

Contentment is nothing but heartfelt, but the eternal soul is never contented. It ever seeks exaltation. Then my heart looked upon the life of beauty and said, "Thou art all knowledge.

Enlighten me as to the mystery of woman." And the life of beauty answered, "O human heart, woman is your own reflection, and whatever you are, she is. Wherever you live, she lives. She is like religion, if not interpreted by the ignorant. And like a moon, if not veiled with clouds. And like a breeze, if not poisoned with impurities."

And my heart walked toward knowledge, the daughter of love and beauty and said, "Bestow upon me wisdom that I might share it with the people."

And she responded, "Say not wisdom, but rather fortune, for real fortune does not come from outside, but begins inside in the holy of holies of life.

"Share of thyself with the people."

4

A Life Apart: Wisdom from the Solitude

Alone, together? Independence, relationship? We benefit from taking time out from everyday life, finding wisdom in an inner search, resting in the arms of nature.

Solitude

Solitude has soft, silky hands
but strong fingers.
It grasps the heart and
makes it ache with sorrow.

Solitude is the ally of sorrow
as well as a companion
of spiritual exaltation.

Beyond My Solitude

Beyond my solitude lies another solitude. To the one who dwells there, my aloneness is a crowded marketplace and my silence a confusion of sounds.

Too young am I, and too restless, to seek that further solitude. The voices of yonder valley still hold my ears, and its shadows bar my way. And I cannot go.

Beyond these hills lies a grove of enchantment, and to the one who dwells there, my peace is but a whirlwind and my enchantment an illusion.

Too young am I, and too riotous, to seek that sacred grove. The taste of blood is clinging in my mouth, and the bow and arrows of my ancestors still linger in my hands. And I cannot go.

Beyond this burdened self lives my freer self. To that self my dreams are a battle fought in twilight, and my desires are the rattling of bones.

Too young am I, and too outraged, to be my freer self.

And how shall I become my freer self unless I slay my burdened selves, or unless all people become free?

How shall the eagle in me soar against the sun until my fledglings leave the nest that I, with my own beak, have built for them?

I Am Not What I Seem

My friend, I am not what I seem.

Seeming is but a garment I wear—a care-woven garment that protects me from your questions and you from my negligence.

The "I" in me, my friend, dwells in the house of silence, and there it shall remain forever—unperceived, unapproachable.

I would not have you believe in what I say or trust in what I do—for my words are nothing but your own thoughts in sound, and my deeds your own hopes in action.

When you say "The wind blows eastward," I say "Aye, it does blow eastward." For I would not have you know that my mind does not dwell upon the wind but upon the sea.

You cannot understand my seafaring thoughts, nor would I have you understand. I would be at sea alone.

When it is day with you, my friend, it is night with me. Yet even then I speak of the noontide that dances upon the hills and of the purple shadow that steals its way across the valley. For you cannot hear the songs of my darkness or see my wings beating against the stars. And I would rather not have you hear or see. I would be with night alone.

When you ascend to your heaven, I descend to my hell. Even then you call to me from across the unbridgeable gulf, "My companion, my comrade!" And I call back to you, "My comrade, my companion!" For I would not have you see my hell. The flame would burn your eyesight, and the smoke would crowd your nostrils. And I love my hell too well to have you visit it. I would be in hell alone.

You love truth and beauty and righteousness. And for your sake I say it is well and seemly to love these things. But in my heart I laugh at your love. Yet I would not have you see my laughter. I would laugh alone.

My friend, you are good and cautious and wise. Nay, you are perfect. And I too speak with you wisely and cautiously. And yet I am mad. But I mask my madness. I would be mad alone.

My friend, you are not my friend, but how shall I make you understand? My path is not your path, yet together we walk, hand in hand.

There Is a Space

There is a space between
one's imagination
and one's attainment
that may only be traversed
by one's longing.

Paradise is there
behind that door
in the next room,
but I have lost the key.

Perhaps I have only mislaid it.

YOUR HOUSE IS YOUR LARGER BODY

Build of your imaginings a bower in the wilderness before you build a house within city walls.

For even as you have homecomings in your twilight, so has the wanderer within you, the ever-distant and alone.

Your house is your larger body.

It grows in the sun and sleeps in the stillness of the night. And it is not dreamless. Does not your house dream, and dreaming, leave the city for grove or hilltop?

Would that I could gather your houses into my hand and like a sower scatter them in forest and meadow!

Would that the valleys were your streets and the green paths your alleys! Then you might seek one another through vineyards and come with the fragrance of the earth in your garments.

But these things are not yet to be.

In their fear your ancestors gathered you too near together. And that fear shall endure a little longer.

A little longer shall your city walls separate your hearths from your fields.

SEEDS OF A TENACIOUS PLANT

We wanderers, ever seeking the lonelier way,
begin no day where we have ended the pre-
vious one.

And no sunrise finds us where sunset left us.
Even while the earth sleeps we travel.

We are the seeds of a tenacious plant,
and it is in our ripeness and in our fullness of
heart
that we are given to the wind and scattered.

Dwelling in Rhythmic Silence

When you can no longer dwell in the solitude of your heart, you live in your lips, and sound is a diversion and a pastime.

And in much of your talking, thinking is half murdered.

For thought is a bird of space that in a cage of words may indeed unfold its wings but cannot fly.

There are those among you who seek the talkative through fear of being alone.

The silence of aloneness reveals to their eyes their naked selves, and they would escape.

And there are those who talk and without knowledge or forethought reveal a truth that they themselves do not understand.

And there are those who have the truth within them, but they tell it not in words.

In the bosom of such as these, the spirit dwells in rhythmic silence.

Only the Naked Live in the Sun

On a morning when the sun was high, one of the disciples—one of those three who had played with him in childhood—approached him saying, "Master, my garment is worn, and I have no other. Give me leave to go to the marketplace and bargain, that perchance I may procure me new raiment."

Almustafa looked upon the young man and said, "Give me your garment." And he did so and stood naked in the noonday.

And, in a voice that was like a young steed running upon a road, Almustafa said:

Only the naked live in the sun. Only the artless ride the wind. And only the one who loses the way a thousand times shall have a homecoming.

The angels are tired of the clever. It was but yesterday that an angel said to me, "We created hell for those who glitter. What else but fire can erase a shining surface and melt a thing to its core?"

And I said, "But in creating hell you created devils to govern hell." The angel answered, "Nay, hell is governed by those who do not yield to fire."

Wise angel! He knows the ways of human beings and the ways of half-human beings. He is one of the seraphim who come to minister to the prophets when they are tempted by the clever. And no doubt he smiles when the prophets smile and weeps also when they weep.

My friends and my mariners, only the naked live in the sun. Only the rudderless can sail the greater sea. Only the one who is dark with the night shall wake with the dawn, and only the one who sleeps with the roots under the snow shall reach the spring.

For you are like roots, and like roots you are simple, yet you have wisdom from the earth. And you are silent, yet you have within your unborn branches the choir of the four winds.

You are frail and you are formless. Yet you are the beginning of giant oaks and of the half-pencilled patterns of the willows against the sky.

Hunter and Hunted

I hunted only your
larger selves that walk the sky.

But the hunter was also the hunted,
for many of the arrows left my bow
only to seek my own breast.

And the flier was also the creeper.
For when my wings were spread in the sun,
their shadow upon the earth was a turtle.

And I, the believer, was also the doubter.
For often I have put my finger
in my own wound that I might have
the greater belief in you
and the greater knowledge of you.

And it is with this belief
and this knowledge that I say:
you are not enclosed within your bodies,
nor confined to houses or fields.

That which is you
dwells above the mountain
and roves with the wind.

It is not a thing that
crawls into the sun for warmth or
digs holes into darkness for safety,
but a thing free,
a spirit that envelops the earth
and moves in the ether.

THE MOUNTAINOUS SPIRIT

The disciple Nathaniel remembers Jesus:

They say that Jesus of Nazareth was humble and meek.

They say that, though he was a just man and righteous, he was a weakling and often confounded by the strong and the powerful. And that when he stood before people of authority, he was but a lamb among lions.

But I say that Jesus had authority over all and knew his power and proclaimed it among the hills of Galilee and in the cities of Judea and Phoenicia.

What man, yielding and soft, would say, "I am life, and I am the way to truth?"

What man, meek and lowly, would say, "I am in God our Father, and our God the Father is in me?"

What man, unmindful of his own strength, would say, "He who believes not in me believes not in this life nor in the life everlasting?"

What man, uncertain of tomorrow, would proclaim, "Your world shall pass away and be nothing but scattered ashes before my words shall pass away?"

Was he doubtful of himself when he said to those who would confound him with a harlot, "He who is without sin, let him cast a stone?"

Did he fear authority when he drove the money changers from the court of the temple, though they were licensed by the priests?

Were his wings shorn when he cried aloud, "My kingdom is above your earthly kingdoms?"

Was he seeking shelter in words when he repeated again and yet again, "Destroy this temple and I will rebuild it in three days?"

Was it a coward who shook his hand in the face of the authorities and pronounced them "liars, low, filthy, and degenerate?"

Shall a man bold enough to say these things to those who ruled Judea be deemed meek and humble?

Nay. The eagle builds not its nest in the weeping willow. And the lion seeks not its den among the ferns.

I am sickened and the bowels within me stir and rise when I hear the fainthearted call Jesus humble and meek that they may justify their own faintheartedness. And when the downtrodden, for comfort and companionship, speak of Jesus as a worm shining by their side.

Yea, my heart is sickened by such people. It is the mighty hunter I would preach, and the mountainous spirit unconquerable.

Finding God

Two men were walking in the valley, and one man pointed with his finger toward the mountainside and said, "Do you see that hermitage? There lives a man who has long divorced the world. He only seeks God and nothing else upon this earth."

And the other man said, "He shall not find God until he leaves the aloneness of his hermitage and returns to our world to share our joy and pain, to dance with our dancers at the wedding feast and to weep with those who weep around the coffins of our dead."

And the other man was convinced in his heart, though in spite of his conviction he answered, "I agree with all that you say, yet I believe the hermit is a good man. And may it not well be that one good man, by his absence, does better than the seeming goodness of these many others by their presence?"

A Voice from the Storm

The hermit Yusuf El Fakhri continued walking back and forth across the room in agitation while I was pondering his sayings and meditating on his description of society's gaping wounds. I ventured again a tactful criticism.

"I hold the utmost regard for your opinion and intentions, and I envy and respect your solitude and aloneness, but I know that this miserable nation has sustained a great loss in your expatriation, for she is in need of an understanding healer to help her through her difficulties and awaken her spirit."

He shook his head slowly and said, "This nation is like all nations. And the people are made of the same element and do not vary except in their exterior appearance, which is of no consequence. The misery of our Eastern nations is the misery of the world, and what you call civilization in the West is nothing but another specter of the many phantoms of tragic deception.

"Hypocrisy will always remain, even if her fingertips are colored and polished. And deceit will never change even if its touch becomes soft and delicate. And falsehood will never turn into truth even if you dress it with silken robes and place it in the palace. And greed will not become contentment, nor will crime become virtue. And eternal slavery to teachings, to customs, and to history will remain slavery even if it paints its face and disguises its voice. Slavery will remain slavery in all its horrible forms, even if it calls itself liberty.

"No, my brother, the West is not higher than the East, nor is the West lower than the East. And the difference that stands between the two is not greater than the difference between the tiger and the lion.

"There is a just and perfect law that I have found behind the exterior of society, a law that equalizes misery, prosperity, and ignorance. It does not prefer one nation to another, nor does it oppress one tribe in order to enrich another."

I exclaimed, "Then civilization is vanity, and all in it is vanity!"

He quickly responded, "Yes, civilization is vanity and all in it is vanity. Inventions and discoveries are but amusements and comforts for the body when it is tired and weary. The conquest of distance and the victory over the seas are but false fruits that do not satisfy the soul or nourish the heart or lift the spirit, for they are far from nature. And those structures and theories that people call knowledge and art are nothing but shackles and golden chains that people drag, rejoicing in their glittering reflections and ringing sounds. They are strong cages whose bars people began fabricating ages ago unaware that, building from the inside, they would soon become prisoners to eternity. Yes, vain are the deeds of humanity, and vain are its purposes, and all is vanity upon the earth."

He paused then slowly added, "And among all vanities of life, there is only one thing that the spirit loves and craves. One thing, dazzling and alone."

"What is it?" I inquired.

He looked at me for a long minute and then closed his eyes. He placed his hands on his chest while his face brightened and with a serene and sincere voice he said,

"It is an awakening in the spirit. It is an awakening in the inner depths of the heart. It is an overwhelming and magnificent power that descends suddenly upon our conscience and opens our eyes.

"We then see life amid a dizzying shower of brilliant music, surrounded by a circle of great light, with humanity standing as a pillar of beauty between the earth and the firmament. It is a flame that suddenly rages within the spirit and sears and purifies the heart, ascending above the earth and hovering in the spacious sky.

"It is a kindness that envelops the individual's heart, whereby one can bewilder and disprove all who oppose it, and revolt against those who refuse to understand its great meaning. It is a secret hand that removed the veil from my eyes while I was a member of society, amidst my family, my friends, and my countrypeople.

"Many times I wondered and asked myself, 'What is this universe, and why am I different from those people who are looking at me.

And how do I know them, and where did I meet them, and why am I living among them? Am I a stranger among them, or is it they who are strange to this earth built by life, which entrusted me with its keys?'"

He suddenly became silent, as if remembering something he had seen long before, refusing to reveal it. Then he stretched his arms forward and whispered, "That is what happened to me four years ago when I left the world and came to this wild place to live in the wide-awakeness of life and enjoy kind thoughts and beautiful silence."

He walked toward the door, looking at the depths of the darkness as if preparing to address the tempest. But he spoke in a vibrating voice saying, "It is an awakening within the spirit. The one who knows it is unable to reveal it by words. And the one who knows it not will never think upon the compelling and beautiful mystery of existence."

An hour had passed, and Yusuf El Fakhri was striding about the room, stopping at random and gazing at the tremendous gray skies. I remained silent, reflecting upon the strange unison of joy and sorrow in his solitary life.

Later in the night he approached me and stared long into my face, as if wanting to commit to memory the picture of the man to whom he had disclosed the piercing secrets of his life. My mind was heavy with turmoil, my eyes with mist. He said quietly, "I am going now to walk through the night with the tempest to feel the closeness of nature's expression. It is a practice that I enjoy greatly in autumn and winter. Here is the wine, and there is the tobacco. Please accept my home as your own for the night."

He wrapped himself in a black robe and added smilingly, "I beg you to fasten the door against intruding people when you leave in the morning, for I plan to spend the day in the forest of the Holy Cedars."

Then he walked toward the door carrying a long walking staff, and he concluded, "If the tempest surprises you again while you are in this vicinity, do not hesitate to take refuge in this hermitage. I hope you will teach yourself to love and not to fear the tempest. Good night, my brother."

He opened the door and walked out into the dark with his head high. I stood at the door to see which course he had taken, but he disappeared from view. For a few minutes I heard the fall of his feet upon the broken stones of the valley.

Morning came after a night of deep thought, and the tempest had passed away, while the sky was clear and the mountains and the plains were reveling in the sun's warm rays. On my way back to the city I felt the spiritual awakening of which Yusuf El Fakhri had spoken, and it was raging throughout every fiber of my being. I felt that my shivering must be visible. And when I felt calm again, all about me was beauty and perfection.

As soon as I reached the crowds of people and heard their voices and saw their deeds, I stopped and said within myself,

"Yes, the spiritual awakening is the most essential thing in one's life, and it is the sole purpose of being. Is not civilization, in all its tragic forms, a supreme motive for spiritual awakening? Then how can we deny existing matter, while its very existence is unwavering proof of its conformability into the intended fitness? The present civilization may possess a vanishing purpose, but the eternal law has offered to that purpose a ladder whose steps can lead to a free substance."

I never saw Yusuf El Fakhri again, for through my endeavors to attend to the ills of civilization, life had expelled me from north Lebanon in late autumn of that same year, and I was required to live in exile in a distant country, whose tempests are domestic.

And leading a hermit's life in that country is a sort of glorious madness, for its society too is ailing.

5

Wisdom Beyond Words

Intense life experiences can stop us in our tracks, and we find that words reach their limit. We can only travel further by pointing silently to a goal that lies beyond the horizon. And then moving in that direction.

Talkative Faults

My loneliness was born
when people praised
my talkative faults and
blamed my silent virtues.

To Write or Not to Write?

Should you care to write (and only the saints know why you should!) you need to have knowledge and art and magic: the knowledge of the music of words, the art of being artless, and the magic of loving your readers.

If I were to choose between the power of writing a poem and the ecstasy of a poem unwritten, I would choose the ecstasy. It is better poetry. But you and all my neighbors agree that I always choose badly.

Should a tree write its autobiography it would not be unlike the history of a race.

Once I said to a poet, "We shall not know your worth until you die."

And he answered saying, "Yes, death is always the revealer. And if indeed you would know my worth, it is that I have more in my heart than upon my tongue, and more in my desire than in my hand."

Surface and Depth

Though the wave of words
is forever upon us,
yet our depth is
forever silent.

The Problem with the Eye

Said the eye one day, "Beyond these valleys I see a mountain veiled with blue mist. Is it not beautiful?"

The ear listened, and after listening intently awhile said, "But where is any mountain? I do not hear it."

Then the hand spoke and said, "I am trying in vain to feel it or touch it, but I can find no mountain."

And the nose said, "There is no mountain, I cannot smell it."

Then the eye turned the other way, and they all began to talk together about the eye's strange delusion.

And they said, "Something must be the matter with the eye."

Four Frogs

Four frogs sat upon a log that lay floating on the edge of a river. Suddenly the log was caught by the current and swept slowly down the stream. The frogs were delighted and absorbed, for never before had they sailed.

At length the first frog spoke and said, "This is indeed a most marvellous log. It moves as if alive. No such log was ever known before!"

Then the second frog spoke and said, "Nay, my friend, the log is like other logs and does not move. It is the river that is walking to the sea and carries us and the log with it."

And the third frog spoke and said, "It is neither the log nor the river that moves. The moving is in our thinking. For without thought nothing moves."

And the three frogs began to wrangle about what was really moving. The quarrel grew hotter and louder, but they could not agree.

Then they turned to the fourth frog, who up to this time had been listening attentively but holding its peace. And they asked its opinion.

And the fourth frog said, "Each of you is right, and none of you is wrong. The moving is in the log and the water and our thinking also."

And the three frogs became very angry, for none of them was willing to admit that its truth was not the whole truth and that the other two were not wholly wrong.

Then a strange thing happened. The three frogs got together and pushed the fourth frog off the log into the river.

LIMITATIONS

If you can see only
what light reveals
and hear only
what sound announces,
then in truth
you do not see
nor do you hear.

THE LAST WATCH

At the high tide of night, when the first breath of dawn came upon the wind, the Forerunner—he who calls himself an echo to a voice yet unheard—left his bedchamber and ascended to the roof of his house.

Long he stood and looked down upon the slumbering city. Then he raised his head and, even as if the sleepless spirits of all those asleep had gathered around him, he opened his lips and said:

My friends and neighbors and you who daily pass my gate, I would speak to you in your sleep, and in the valley of your dreams I would walk naked and unrestrained. For heedless are your waking hours and deaf are your sound-burdened ears.

Long did I love you, and overmuch. I love each among you as though that one were all, and all of you as if you were a single one. In the spring of my heart I sang in your gardens, and in the summer of my heart I watched at your threshing floors.

Yes, I loved you all, the giant and the pygmy, the leper and the anointed, the ones who grope in the dark and the ones who dance their days upon the mountains.

You the strong have I loved, though the marks of your iron hoofs are yet upon my flesh. And you the weak, though you have drained my faith and wasted my patience.

You the rich have I loved, while bitter was your honey to my mouth. And you the poor, though you knew my empty-handed shame.

You the poet with the bowed lute and blind fingers—you have I loved in self-indulgence. And you the scholar, ever gathering rotted shrouds in potters' fields.

You the priest I have loved, who sits in the silences of yesterday, questioning the fate of my tomorrow. And you the worshippers of gods who are the images of your own desires.

You the thirsting woman whose cup is ever full, I have loved you in understanding. And you the woman of restless nights, you too I have loved in pity.

You the talkative have I loved saying, "Life hath much to say." And you the dumb have I loved, whispering to myself, "Says this one not in silence that which I would gladly hear in words?"

And you the judge and the critic I have loved also. Yet when you have seen me crucified you said, "He bleeds rhythmically, and the pattern his blood makes upon his white skin is beautiful to behold."

Yes, I have loved you all—the young and the old, the trembling reed and the oak.

But alas, it was the over-abundance of my heart that turned you from me. You would drink love from a cup but not from a surging river. You would hear love's faint murmur, but when love shouts, you would muffle your ears.

And because I have loved you all, you have said, "Too soft and yielding is his heart, and too undiscerning is his path. It is the love of a needy one who picks crumbs even as he sits at kingly feasts. And it is the love of a weakling, for the strong loves only the strong."

And because I have loved you overmuch you have said, "It is but the love of a blind person who knows not the beauty of one nor the ugliness of another. And it is thc love of the tasteless who drinks vinegar even as wine. And it is the love of the impertinent and the overweening, for what stranger could be our mother and father and sister and brother?"

This you have said, and more.

Often in the marketplace you pointed your fingers at me and said mockingly, "There goes the ageless one, the man without seasons, who at the noon hour plays games with our children and at eventide sits with our elders and assumes wisdom and understanding."

And I said to myself, "I will love them more. Aye, even more. I will hide my love with the semblance of hate and disguise my tenderness as bitterness. I will wear an iron mask, and only when armed and mailed shall I seek them."

Then I laid a heavy hand upon your bruises, and like a tempest in the night I thundered in your ears. From the housetop I proclaimed you hypocrites, pharisees, tricksters—false and empty earth-bubbles.

The short-sighted among you I cursed for blind bats, and those too near the earth I likened to soulless moles.

The eloquent I pronounced fork-tongued, the silent stone-lipped. And the simple and artless I called the dead who never weary of death.

The seekers after worldly knowledge I condemned as offenders of the holy spirit. And those who would have nothing but the spirit I branded hunters of shadows who cast their nets in flat waters and catch but their own images.

Thus with my lips I denounced you while my heart, bleeding within me, called you tender names.

It was love lashed by its own self that spoke. It was pride, half-slain, that fluttered in the dust. It was my hunger for your love that raged from the housetop, while my own love, kneeling in silence, prayed for your forgiveness.

But behold a miracle! It was my disguise that opened your eyes, and my seeming to hate that woke your hearts.

And now you love me.

You love the swords that stroke you and the arrows that crave your breast. It comforts you to be wounded, and only when you drink of your own blood can you be intoxicated.

Like moths that seek destruction in the flame, you gather daily in my garden. With faces uplifted and eyes enchanted, you watch me tear the fabric of your days. And in whispers you say one to another, "He sees with the light of God. He speaks like the prophets of old. He unveils our souls and unlocks our hearts, and like the eagle that knows the way of foxes he knows our ways."

Aye, in truth I know your ways, but only as an eagle knows the ways of its fledglings. And I would gladly disclose my secret. Yet in my need for your nearness I feign remoteness, and in fear of the ebb tide of your love I guard the flood-gates of my love.

After saying these things the Forerunner covered his face with his hands and wept bitterly. For he knew in his heart that love, humiliated in its nakedness, is greater than love that seeks triumph in disguise. And he was ashamed.

But suddenly he raised his head, and like one waking from sleep he outstretched his arms and said:

Night is over,
and we children of night
must die
when dawn comes
leaping upon the hills.

And out of our ashes
a mightier love shall rise.
And it shall laugh in the sun,
and it shall be deathless.

Shall I Sing?

They were silent, awaiting his word, but Almustafa answered them not.

For the sadness of memory was upon him, and he said in his heart:

Have I said that I shall sing?
Nay, I can only open my lips
that the voice of life may come forth
and go out to the wind
for joy and support.

The Stream Has Reached the Sea

Patient, over-patient,
is the captain of my ship.

The wind blows,
and restless are the sails.
Even the rudder begs direction.

Yet quietly my captain
awaits my silence.

And these my mariners,
who have heard the choir
of the greater sea,
they too have heard me patiently.

Now they shall wait no longer.
I am ready.

The stream has reached the sea,
and once more the great mother
holds her son against her breast.

The Word of Longing

In his old age, the beloved disciple John talks about why he called Jesus the "Word" in his gospel:

You ask why I call him the first Word.

Listen and I will answer:

In the beginning God moved in space, and out of God's measureless stirring, the earth was born and the seasons thereof.

Then God moved again, and life streamed forth. And the longing of life sought the height and the depth and would have more of itself.

Then God spoke this longing, and those words were humanity, and humanity was a spirit begotten by God's spirit.

And when God spoke this way, the Christ was the first Word and that Word was perfect. And when Jesus of Nazareth came to the world, the first Word was spoken to us, and the sound was made flesh and blood.

Jesus the anointed was the first Word of God uttered unto humanity, even as if one apple tree in an orchard should bud and blossom a day before the other trees. And in God's orchard, that day was an aeon.

We are all sons and daughters of the Most High, but the anointed one was God's first-born, who dwelt in the body of Jesus of Nazareth. He walked among us and we beheld him.

All this I say that you may understand, not only in the mind but rather in the spirit.

The mind weighs and measures,
but it is the spirit that
reaches the heart of life and
embraces the secret.
And the seed of the spirit is deathless.

The wind may blow and then cease,
and the sea shall swell and then weary,
but the heart of life is a sphere,
quiet and serene,
and the star that shines therein
is fixed forevermore.

Let Your Longing Pronounce the Words

The disciple Matthew remembers an encounter with Jesus:

I said to Jesus, "I would pray this moment, yet my tongue is heavy. Teach me to pray."

And Jesus said, "When you would pray, let your longing pronounce the words. It is in my longing now to pray thus:

"Our Father in earth and heaven,
sacred is thy name.
Thy will be done with us, even as in space.
Give us of thy bread, sufficient for the day.
In thy compassion forgive us and
enlarge us to forgive one another.
Guide us towards thee and
stretch down thy hand to us in darkness.
For thine is the kingdom,
and in thee is our power and our fulfillment."

It was now evening, and Jesus walked down from the hills, and all of us followed him.

As I followed, I was repeating his prayer and remembering all that he had said. For I knew that the words that had fallen like flakes that day must set and grow firm like crystals.

And that the wings that had fluttered above our heads were to beat the earth like iron hoofs.

The Wings of Vision

Then said a teacher, "Speak to us of teaching."
And Almustafa said:

No one can reveal to you anything but that which already lies half asleep in the dawning of your knowledge.

The teachers who walk in the shadow of the temple among their followers give not of their wisdom but rather of their faith and love.

If they are indeed wise, they do not bid you enter the house of their wisdom, but rather lead you to the threshold of your own mind.

Astronomers may speak to you of their understanding of space, but they cannot give you their understanding.

Musicians may sing to you of the rhythm that is in all space, but they cannot give you the ear that catches the rhythm, nor the voice that echoes it.

And the one who is versed in the science of numbers can tell of the regions of weight and measure, but cannot conduct you there.

For the vision of one person lends not its wings to that of another.

And even as each one of you stands alone in God's knowledge, so must each one of you be alone in your knowledge of God and in your understanding of the earth.

Two Learned Men

Once there lived in the ancient city of Afkar two learned men who hated and belittled each other's learning. For one of them denied the existence of the gods, and the other was a believer.

One day the two met in the marketplace. Among their followers they began to dispute and argue about the existence or non-existence of the gods. And after hours of contention they parted.

That evening the unbeliever went to the temple and prostrated himself before the altar and prayed to the gods to forgive his wayward past.

And the same hour the other learned man, who had upheld the gods, burned his sacred books. For he had become an unbeliever.

I Came to Remove Your Wisdom

I only speak to you in words that which you yourselves know in thought.

And what is word-knowledge but a shadow of wordless knowledge?

Your thoughts and my words are waves from a sealed memory that keeps records of our yesterdays, of the ancient days when the earth knew neither us nor herself and of the nights when earth was being formed with confusion.

Wise men have come to you to give you of their wisdom.

I came to remove your wisdom.

Doctrines

Many a doctrine is
like a window pane.
We see truth through it
but it divides us from truth.

Disclosing the Power to Rise

A Greek apothecary remembers Jesus:

He made whole those who were afflicted with diseases unknown to the Greeks and the Egyptians. They say he even called the dead back to life. And whether this be true or not true, it declares his power. For only to him who has wrought great things is the greatest ever attributed.

They say also that Jesus visited India and the country between the Two Rivers,[2] and that there the priests revealed to him the knowledge of all that is hidden in the recesses of our flesh.

Yet that knowledge may have been given to him directly by the gods and not through the priests. For that which has remained unknown to all people for an aeon may be disclosed to one person in but a moment. And Apollo may lay

2. Ancient Mesopotamia, the "two rivers" being the Tigris and Euphrates.

his hand on the heart of the obscure and make it wise.

Many doors were open to the Tyrians and the Thebans, and to this man also certain sealed doors were opened. He entered the temple of the soul, which is the body. He beheld the evil spirits that conspire against our sinews and also the good spirits that spin the threads thereof.

I think it was by the power of opposition and resistance that he healed the sick, but in a manner unknown to our philosophers. He astonished fever with his snow-like touch, and it retreated. He surprised hardened limbs with his own calm, and they yielded to him and were at peace.

He knew the ebbing sap within the furrowed bark, but how he reached the sap with his fingers I do not know. He knew the sound steel underneath the rust, but how he freed the sword and made it shine no one can tell.

Sometimes it seems to me that he heard the murmuring pain of all things that grow in the sun. And that then he lifted them up and supported them, not only by his own knowledge, but also by disclosing to them their own power to rise and become whole.

Singing Your Lost Dreaming

Let him who would have wisdom
seek it in a buttercup or
in a pinch of red clay.

I am still the singer.
I shall sing the earth,
and I shall sing your lost dreaming,
which walks the day
between sleep and sleep.

When Wisdom Ceases to Be Wisdom

Wisdom ceases to be wisdom
when it becomes
too proud to weep,
too grave to laugh,
and too full of its self to
seek other than itself.

A Love Song in the Wind

Cleopas of Bethroune[3] remembers the words of Jesus:

When Jesus spoke, the whole world was hushed to listen. His words were not for our ears but rather for the elements of which God made this earth.

He spoke to the sea, our vast mother who gave us birth. He spoke to the mountain, our elder brother whose summit is a promise.

And he spoke to the angels beyond the sea and the mountain, to whom we entrusted our dreams before the clay in us was made hard in the sun.

Still his speech slumbers within our breast like a love song half forgotten, and sometimes it burns itself through to our memory.

---

3. Cleopas was one of the two disciples who encountered Jesus after the resurrection on the road to Emmaus as related in the Gospel of Luke, chapter 24.

His speech was simple and joyous, and the sound of his voice was like cool water in a land of drought.

Once he raised his hand against the sky, and his fingers were like the branches of a sycamore tree. And he said with a great voice:

"The prophets of old have spoken to you, and your ears are filled with their speech. But I say unto you, empty your ears of what you have heard."

And these words of Jesus, "But I say unto you . . . " were not uttered by a man of our race nor of our world, but rather by a host of seraphim marching across the sky of Judea.

Again and yet again he would quote the law and the prophets, and then he would say, "But I say unto you. . . ."

O what burning words, what waves of seas unknown to the shores of our mind! "But I say unto you. . . ."

What stars seeking the darkness of the soul, and what sleepless souls awaiting the dawn!

To tell of the speech of Jesus one must needs have his speech or the echo thereof. I have neither the speech nor the echo.

I beg you to forgive me for beginning a story that I cannot end. But the end is not yet upon my lips. It is still a love song in the wind.

I Go with the Wind

If anything I have said is truth,
that truth shall reveal itself in a clearer voice
and in words more akin to your thoughts.

I go with the wind, people of Orphalese,
but not down into emptiness.
And if this day is not a fulfilment
of your needs and my love,
then let it be a promise till another day.

Humanity's needs change
but not its love,
nor its desire that its love
should satisfy its needs.

Know therefore that
from the greater silence
I shall return.

The mist that drifts away at dawn,
leaving but dew in the fields,
shall rise and gather into a cloud
and then fall down again in rain.
And not unlike the mist have I been.

In the stillness of the night
I have walked in your streets,
and my spirit has entered your houses.
And your heartbeats were in my heart,
and your breath was upon my face,
and I knew you all.

Aye, I knew your joy and your pain,
and in your sleep,
your dreams were my dreams.

And oftentimes I was among you,
a lake among the mountains.
I mirrored the summits in you,
and the bending slopes,
and even the passing flocks
of your thoughts and your desires.

And to my silence came
the laughter of your children in streams,
and the longing of your youths in rivers.
And when they reached my depth,
the streams and the rivers
ceased not yet to sing.

But something still sweeter than laughter
and greater than longing came to me.

It was the boundless in you—
the vast being in whom
you are all but cells and sinews,
the voice in whose chant
all your singing is
but a soundless throbbing.

It is in that vast human being
that you are vast,
and in beholding that one
that I beheld you and loved you.

Like a giant oak tree
covered with apple blossoms
is that vast one in you.
Its might binds you to the earth,
its fragrance lifts you into space,
and in its durability,
you are deathless.

If, in the twilight of memory,
we should meet once more,
we shall speak again together,
and you shall sing to me
a deeper song.

And if our hands should meet
in another dream,
we shall build another
tower in the sky.

Sources of the Selections

Spirits Rebellious (1908) SR
The Broken Wings (1912) BW
A Tear and A Smile (1914) TS
"Dead Are My People" (1916) DP
The Procession (1918) TP
The Madman (1918) M
The Forerunner (1920) F
The Tempest (1920) T
"Your Thought and Mine" (1920s) YT
"History and the Nation" (1920) HN
The Prophet (1923) P
The New Frontier (1925) NF

Sand and Foam (1926) SF
Jesus The Son of Man (1928) JSM
The Earth Gods (1931) EG
The Wanderer (1932) W
The Garden of the Prophet (1933) GP
Lazarus and His Beloved (1933) LB

Living a Wise Life

Nirvana (SF)
To Be a Garden Without Walls (GP)
There Lived a Man (SF)
The Other (SF)
Eating and Drinking (P)
Gatekeeper of Your Necessities (JSM)
"Nicodemus The Poet"
When You Work With Love (P)
The Wisdom of Critics (F)
The Scholar and the Poet (SF)
The Mask of Wit (SF)
Professional Talkers (SF)
Being Candid (SF)
Ancestry (SF)
The Children of Tomorrow (NF)
Your Children (P)
The Best Sacrifice (JSM)
Speaking Less of God (GP)

Community Wisdom

Government (SF)
Between the Frown of the Tiger and the Smile of the Wolf (SR)
Inherited Spiritual Disease (BW)
Good Government (W)
Busy Cattle (SR)
The One Thousand Laws (W)
The Criminal (TS)
Your Thought and Mine (YT)
War and the Small Nations (F)
History and the Shepherdess (HN)
Pity the Nation (GP)
The New Frontiers (NF)
O Liberty (SR)
A Throne Beyond Your Vision (JSM)

Wise Exchanges

A Gracious Wolf (SF)
Credit (SF)
Pomegranates (W)
A Prison of Wealth (BW)
The Song of True Fortune (TS)
Value (F)
In the Marketplace (P)
Giving Without Looking in a Mirror (P)
Generosity and Pride (SF)
Giving as the Myrtle Breathes (P)
Generosity (SF)
None to Receive (SF)
Giving for Those in Need (DP)
The House of Real Fortune (TS)

A Life Apart: Wisdom from the Solitude

Solitude (BW)
Beyond My Solitude (F)
I Am Not What I Seem (M)
There is a Space (SF)
Your House is Your Larger Body (P)
Seeds of a Tenacious Plant (P)
Dwelling in Rhythmic Silence (P)
Only the Naked Live in the Sun (GP)
Hunter and Hunted (P)
The Mountainous Spirit (JSM)
Finding God (W)
A Voice from the Storm (T)

Wisdom Beyond Words

Talkative Faults (SF)
To Write or Not to Write (SF)
Surface and Depth (SF)
The Problem with the Eye (M)
Four Frogs (F)
Limitations (SF)
The Last Watch (F)
Shall I Sing? (GP)
The Stream Has Reached the Sea (P)
The Word of Longing (JSM)
Let Your Longing Pronounce the Words (JSM)
The Wings of Wisdom (P)
Two Learned Men (M)
I Came to Remove Your Wisdom (P)
Doctrines (SF)
Disclosing the Power to Rise (JSM)
Singing Your Lost Dreaming (GP)
When Wisdom Ceases to Be Wisdom (SF)
A Love Song in the Wind (JSM)
I Go With the Wind (P)

About the Author

Dates from the life of Gibran Khalil Gibran, the author's full Arabic name, which due to a registration spelling mistake at his first school in the United States was changed from the usual spelling to "Kahlil."

1883: Born in Bsharri, a village in the north of Lebanon.

1895: Gibran's mother immigrates to Boston with her four children, hoping to flee poverty and unhappiness, while her husband remains in Lebanon, imprisoned for embezzling from the government.

1898: Returns to Lebanon to study Arabic and French at a Maronite-run preparatory school in Beirut. By some accounts his mother wants to remove him from unsavory artistic influences in Boston.

1902: Returns to Boston. In fifteen months' time, he loses his mother, sister, and half-brother to tuberculosis.

1904: Through photographer Fred Holland Day he meets Mary Haskell, a school headmistress who becomes his patron, muse, editor, and possible lover. Publishes several poems in prose gathered later under the title *A Tear and a Smile.*

1908–10: Funded by Mary, he attends art school in Paris.

1911: Settles in New York where he starts an intimate correspondence with May Ziadeh, a Lebanese intellectual living in Cairo.

1918: *The Madman*, Gibran's first book written in English, is published.

1920: Together with other Arab and Lebanese writers and poets living in the United States, he founds a literary society called *Al Rabita al Qalamiyyah* (The Pen Bond).

1923: *The Prophet* is published with immediate success. He begins a friendship with Barbara Young, who later becomes his new muse and editor.

1928: *Jesus The Son of Man* is published.

1931: Dies in a hospital in New York at the age of 48, due to cirrhosis of the liver. As was his wish, Gibran's body is transferred in 1932 to Lebanon and is buried in his native town of Bsharri. An old monastery is purchased, which becomes a museum to his memory.

These bare facts belie the complexity and turbulence of Kahlil Gibran's life, both inner and outer. As one of his biographers, Suheil Bushrui, writes:

"The more that has been written about Gibran the more elusive the man himself has tended to become as critics, friends, and biographers have built up a variety of unconnected pictures. Gibran himself is partly to blame. He wrote very little about his own life and in recurrent moments of insecurity and 'vagueness,' particularly during his first years of recognition, often fabricated or embellished his humble origins and troubled background. This self-perpetuation of his myth—a tendency followed by other literary figures such as Yeats and Swift—was not intellectual dishonesty, but a manifestation of the poetic mind's desire to create its own mythology" (Bushrui, 1998).

A good online biography can be found at the website of the Gibran National Committee: *www.gibrankhalilgibran.org*

As Bushrui notes, the many biographies and biographical studies of Gibran do not agree on many points. They are very much like the different voices presented in Gibran's book *Jesus, The*

Son of Man, each reporting various facets of a person who embraced both the highs and lows, the lights and shadows of a fully human life.

A selection of the biographies and collections of Gibran's letters is below.

Bushrui, S. and J. Jenkins. (1998). *Kahlil Gibran: Man and Poet.* Oxford: Oneworld.

Bushrui, S. and S. H. al-Kuzbari (eds. and trans.) (1995). *Gibran: Love Letters.* Oxford: Oneworld.

Gibran, J. and K. Gibran. (1974). *Kahlil Gibran: His Life and World.* Boston: New York Graphic Society.

Gibran, J. and K. Gibran. (2017). *Kahlil Gibran: Beyond Borders.* (Updated version of the 1974 book). Northampton, MA: Interlink Books.

Hilu, V. (1972). *Beloved Prophet: The Love Letters of Kahlil Gibran and Mary Haskell and Her Private Journal.* New York: Alfred Knopf.

Naimy, M. (1950). *Kahlil Gibran: A Biography.* New York: Philosophical Library.

Waterfield, R. (1998). *Prophet: The Life and Times of Kahlil Gibran*. New York: St Martin's Press.

Young, B. (1945). *This Man from Lebanon: A Study of Kahlil Gibran*. New York: Alfred Knopf.

About the Editor

Photo by William A. Matheiu

Neil Douglas-Klotz, PhD is a renowned writer in the fields of Middle Eastern spirituality and the translation and interpretation of the ancient Semitic languages of Hebrew, Aramaic, and Arabic. Living in Scotland, he directs the Edinburgh Institute for Advanced Learning and for many years was co-chair of the Mysticism Group of the American Academy of Religion.

A frequent speaker and workshop leader, he is the author of several books. His books on the Aramaic spirituality of Jesus include *Prayers of the Cosmos, The Hidden Gospel, Original Meditation: The Aramaic Jesus and the Spirituality of Creation,* and *Blessings of the Cosmos.* His books on a comparative view of "native" Middle Eastern spirituality include *Desert Wisdom: A Nomad's Guide to Life's Big Questions* and *The Tent of Abraham* (with Rabbi Arthur Waskow and Sr. Joan Chittister). His books on Sufi spirituality include *The Sufi Book of Life: 99 Pathways of the Heart for the Modern Dervish* and *A Little Book of Sufi Stories.* His biographical collections of the works of his Sufi teachers include *Sufi Vision and Initiation* (Samuel L. Lewis) and *Illuminating the Shadow* (Moineddin Jablonski). He has also written a mystery novel set in the first century C.E. Holy Land entitled *A Murder at Armageddon.*

For more information about his work, see the website of the Abwoon Network (*www.abwoon .org*) or his Facebook page (*www.facebook.com /AuthorNeilDouglasKlotz/*)

Hampton Roads Publishing Company

. . . for the evolving human spirit

Hampton Roads Publishing Company publishes books on a variety of subjects, including spirituality, health, and other related topics.

For a copy of our latest trade catalog, call (978) 465-0504 or visit our distributor's website at *www.redwheelweiser.com*. You can also sign up for our newsletter and special offers by going to *www.redwheelweiser.com/newsletter/*.